How to teach this unit

Settlements are where people live and work, and are sometimes called communities. We all live somewhere, so the topic has relevance to the whole class. The children may come from a number of widely differing settlements or from one main type such as a suburban estate. This does not matter, as each settlement is interesting in itself, and will have its own story about how and why it was established and how it is changing over time. It is important, however, that children have a chance to experience a different type of place from where they mainly live, but this need not be a long way off: it might be just across the town or in nearby countryside.

The fact that the school is in a community means that fieldwork can, and should, be an important part of children gaining first-hand experience of where they are. You might want to investigate a particular area, or make comparisons with another, or even study a particular street or road in depth through time and space.

It is important to build on what the children may have studied before – local settlements provide a range of opportunities for children of all ages to study, and so it is important for teaching staff to identify the aspects they wish to teach in different year-groups, so that children do not repeat work they have done previously.

It is also important that children have the opportunity to look at a range of settlements in other parts of the world in order to learn that settlements are not just a feature of their own country.

Time allocation

The teaching time available for geography can vary enormously. SuperSchemes units have been written with three possibilities in mind:

- a **short–medium** unit (5–10 hours)
- a **long** unit (10–15 hours)
- a **continuous** unit (15–30 minutes per week).

The medium term plans allow you to choose an appropriate length for your particular class. Some of the longer medium term plans offer enough material for you to continue with the topic later in the year.

This unit may benefit from being taught in a concentrated period of time, as the knowledge and skills learned relate to tasks which follow on from one another. However, there may be a case for making it a whole-day teaching unit, putting the children's maps on display at the end of the day.

Key ideas

Enquiry

The concept of enquiry about settlements underpins all the suggestions for activities and discussions in this unit. Children are encouraged to use a range of resources – books, maps, newspapers, photographs, etc., as well as the internet and first-hand experience – to learn more about a range of places.

How places change over time

This is a key geographical concept, and children should learn not only about their own local environment but also about a range of places, far and near. They need to consider these places through investigating not only differences but also similarities between localities. In many cases, the reasons why places grew up may have changed very little since the days of ancient settlement. However, the function and growth of these settlements will often have changed significantly with respect to the services they provide and the character they exhibit.

Environmental change

All settlements are in a state of change to some extent, and children should learn to recognise how, and in what form, this change is happening. The growth or decline of industry, population migration and the attraction of city life are just some of the interesting factors which affect how a settlement changes over time. For example, what is the effect on a village of losing its public transport? what is the effect of the closure of an industrial complex on its surrounding area?

Research

Wiegand (1993) talks about an experiment in which children between 3 and 5 years old were asked to find a toy elephant in a room. The children were very much at ease with finding their way around the room and searching it. He concluded that children are able to plot routes and find their way from place to place, even from a very early age.

> **References**
>
> DfEE/QCA (1998/2000) *A Scheme of Work for Key Stages 1 and 2*. London: DfEE/QCA.
>
> Wiegand, P. (1993) *Children and Primary Geography*. London: Continuum.

Where do I start?

As the study of settlements relies a great deal on children being able to use a range of maps and atlases, it is important that they feel comfortable using them. They are not expected to use grid references too soon, but should be able to look at a map, identify the main features, including settlements, and relate their location to a variety of physical features. They will consider questions such as:

- How near are these settlements to a river?
- Is there a crossing-point?
- Why do settlements appear to be in a line on the map?
- What influenced their location?
- Are there any examples of places where settlements have expanded into each other and formed a conurbation?

Another good starting point is to look at a range of reading books that highlight a settlement, and to identify what the place is like and why it might have originated here. This helps the children to see that places are real, and are a result of the effects of time, as well as of natural features and human choice.

Introducing the topic

To stimulate children's enthusiasm, it will be useful to:

- Put appropriate vocabulary lists on display.
- Ensure there is a range of colourful maps for children to look at outside the structured lesson. What kind of function do different maps have?
- Encourage children to look up map sites on the internet (examples are given on the CD).
- Develop a number of challenging questions to stimulate thinking skills; for example:
  - How many places are really 'new' in Britain today?
  - What can you find out from a map that you can't find out from visiting the place?
  - If a group were to plan a settlement on a new site today, what would be the most important factors that would influence its location? (e.g. proximity to major city, good transport infrastructure).
  - When is a map not a map? (Show a range of maps, including some pictorial ones, and ask children to decide on what makes a map.)

Concept map

(knowledge-based)

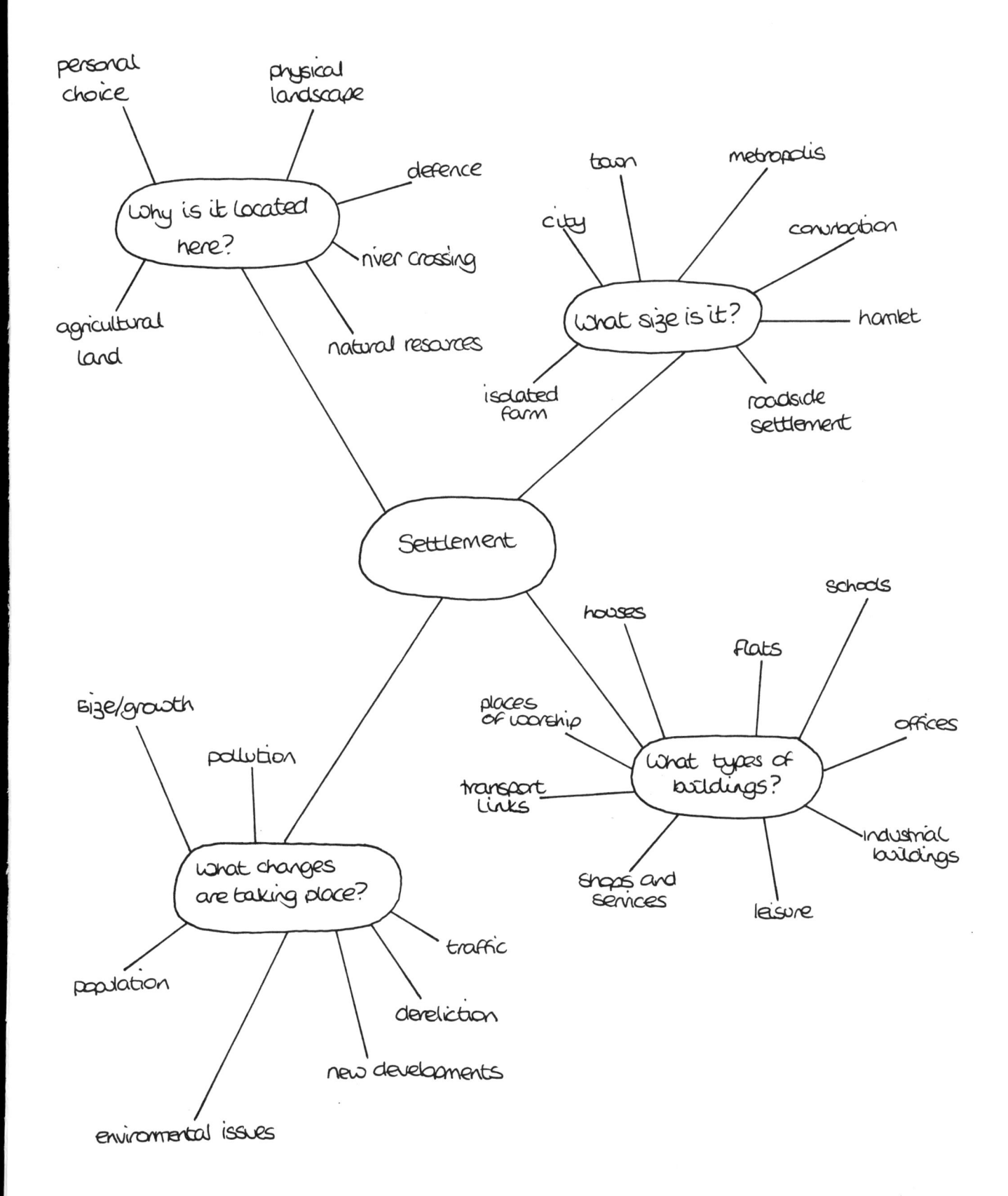

Why is it located here?
- personal choice
- physical landscape
- defence
- river crossing
- natural resources
- agricultural land

What size is it?
- town
- metropolis
- city
- conurbation
- hamlet
- isolated farm
- roadside settlement

Settlement

What types of buildings?
- houses
- schools
- flats
- offices
- places of worship
- transport links
- shops and services
- industrial buildings
- leisure

What changes are taking place?
- size/growth
- pollution
- population
- traffic
- dereliction
- new developments
- environmental issues

SuperSchemes | Unit 9: Village settlers

Medium term plan: Village settlers

Learning outcomes	Key questions	Pupil activities	Resources/ Key vocabulary	Assessment opportunities
To show knowledge and understanding of early settlers and the characteristics of early settlements To recognise that settlements have specific features and are located in response to physical features and human choice To use maps to identify settlements and obtain evidence To know the vocabulary associated with a village.	What makes a good settlement? Where did early settlers choose to live and why? How do settlements develop? What evidence can we find on maps? See lesson plan 1	1 In small groups, discuss what makes a good settlement. Using criteria discussed, find examples on OS maps of settlements which have these features. Explain reasons for choices. See activity sheet 1	OS map extracts *Invaders, settlers, Saxon, Roman, Viking, settlements, flooding, defence, water supply, fuel, building materials*	Can pupils identify a village settlement on a map extract without prompting, and explain why it might have been chosen as a settlement site?
		2 Give out meanings of place names – ton, ham, etc – and discuss origins of place names. Ask pairs of children to identify settlements with these names on map extracts. Differentiate by asking children to list the features of these settlements and to explain why they think the sites were chosen. **Anglo-Saxon place names** ford – river crossing ham – settlement den – hill ton – farm or village wic – farmstead	Definitions of place names and lists of examples OS Map extracts *Features, river-crossing point, route-way*	Do children know the meanings of place names e.g. *East Dereham, Harleston, Docking*?
To identify a variety of map symbols and recognise their meanings To know the characteristics of a village To recognise similarities and differences between places.	What are villages like today? How is a village similar to/different from another type of settlement?	3 Using the map key, identify the symbols used for features within the settlements investigated. Compare the features of different villages and then ask children to suggest alternative symbols. See activity sheet 2	OS maps with key OS map symbol cards – *use associated language*	Do pupils know the meaning of map symbols most commonly used in a village settlement on an OS map when given out of context, e.g. church, telephone box?
To draw a map of the layout of a settlement from a given description To describe the features of the place where the pupils themselves live.	What is this place like? What are the important features which characterize it?	4 Play a tape of someone describing the place to which they have recently moved. Ask the children to draw a sketch map of the place, putting in as much detail as possible. Compare with a published map if possible. As an extension activity, ask the children to describe the place where they live to someone who has never been there. Draft the ideas and then tape-record their description.	Tape recordings of place descriptions OS maps	**Speaking and listening activity** Can pupils draw an accurate sketch map from listening to details? Can they accurately describe the features of the place they live in and indicate how these features are linked together to form a settlement?
To draw a map of a layout of a settlement.	What features does this place have? See lesson plan 2	5 Give children a sheet of paper with a river or other feature marked on it and ask them to design a new village settlement using OS map symbols. Differentiate by specifying to particular groups different features that need to be included, e.g. a small housing estate. Compare and discuss maps.	Copy of OS map symbols or OS map symbol cards	Does the settlement design produced show understanding of the characteristics of a village and a knowledge of map symbols?

Cross-curricular links:
History – Invaders and Settlers unit
Literacy – work on place names/root words; finding, selecting and recording information; communicating findings – speaking and listening
ICT – graphical modelling for village designs
Citizenship – how we can sustain our environments?

Lesson plan 1: Early settlers and settlements

Subject: Geography (year 4)
Time/Duration: one hour

Learning outcomes
In this lesson pupils will learn:

- about early settlers and the characteristics of early settlements
- that settlements have specific features and are located in response to physical features and human choice.

Background to the current lesson
This is the first lesson in this unit of work. The children have previously investigated their own locality and have simple mapping skills.

Lesson details

Introduction (5 minutes)
Ask the children to discuss with a partner what they think the term 'settlement' means, and what they think are the main characteristics of a settlement. Bring the ideas together in the whole class.

Main activity (20 minutes)
Explain to the children that they are going to take on the role of early settlers arriving in the UK. There are no cities or towns, but just a few settlements in which not all of the inhabitants are friendly.

Arrange the children in groups of three or four, give them a large sheet of paper, and ask them to make a list of those things that they think would make a good settlement. You may need to prompt them by suggesting water supply as a starting point.

At the end of the small-group discussion, bring the children together and compile a list of those features that make a good settlement, e.g. supply of building materials, fuel for fire, raised land so that enemies can be spotted, fertile land for farming and/or animals for hunting.

Ask the children to consider the list for a few minutes and then, in their groups, to discuss which they think are the most important. Tell the children to prioritise the features.

Bring the children together and compare the different lists.

Developing the activity (30 minutes)
Now give the children a map extract – at least A3 size. East Anglia or Lincolnshire are good for this exercise.

Ask the children to find examples of settlements on their extract that have any or all of the features discussed.

Record the names of the settlements and the features that each settlement has. Provide an outline grid for those children that need it (see note on **Differentiation** below).

Bring the children together and compare some of the settlements looked at and their features.

> Teaching point – if appropriate, the teacher could interject at some point and ask the children if they know how height is shown on a map, and then explain contour lines in simple terms, pointing out any examples.

Explain to the children that they are now going to decide, in groups, which of the settlements on their extract is the best site. Each group will need to appoint a spokesperson, who will have to give the group's reasons for choosing this particular site.

Plenary (5 minutes)
Discuss (or recap) what the main features of early settlements were, and the advantages and disadvantages of particular sites: for example, a hill-top site might be good for defence, but might also be a long way from supplies of water and wood. Can the children suggest any ways of overcoming these problems?

Differentiation
The children will be arranged in mixed-ability groups for this lesson. It may be that some groups will need a grid to be provided for recording the names of settlements and features.

Resources
- large sheets of paper and pens for each group
- map extracts for each group
- map extract with clear example of contour lines – possibly on OHT.

Cross-curricular links
History – invaders and settlers

Literacy – speaking and listening.

Lesson plan 2: Designing a new village settlement

Subject: Geography (year 4)
Time/Duration: one hour

Learning outcomes
In this lesson, children will learn:

- about the human and physical features of village settlements
- how to draw maps which show the layout of village settlements.

Background to the current lesson
This is the last lesson in the medium term plan. The children have previously investigated early settlements, looked at symbols used on OS maps to represent settlement features, and followed and described different route-ways on maps. Prior to this unit, the children have experience of drawing simple maps of their own localities.

Lesson details
Introduction (15 minutes)
Ask the children to talk with a partner, recapping the features often found in a village. Bring the ideas together in the whole class. (5 minutes)

In the same pairs, ask the children to draw on whiteboards some of the symbols used to show village features on an OS map. Bring the whole class together and compile a list. Make sure that the following have been mentioned: colour of A and B roads, footpath, bridleway, parking, picnic site, bridge, telephone box, church, post office, public house. (10 minutes)

Main activity (40 minutes)
Explain to the children that they are going to design their own village settlement. They will be allowed to choose some of their own features but some will be specified for them. They are to make sure that they put a key on their map and that they use the commonly used OS map symbols. Make sure that you have a number of OS maps available so that the children can use the map keys for reference. This task is differentiated (see **Differentiation** below). (30 minutes – this will probably not be enough time to finish their designs so they will need an additional lesson in which to do this.)

Ask the children, in pairs, to take turns to talk about their settlement designs, explaining the features they have included and why they have located them in particular places. (10 minutes)

Plenary (10 minutes)
Bring the class together and ask them for any similarities and/or differences that they noticed when they were discussing their designs with their partners.

Are there any features that all the children in the class have included – why do they think this is?

Ask them how putting a major road through their settlement would affect it. Who would be affected, and why?

Differentiation
The children will work in mixed-ability pairs for discussion, and in three differentiated groups for the main task:

Below average group: this group may need some of the OS map symbols transferred onto a separate sheet for ease of use.

Average group: they are to use the OS map keys for reference and must include a small housing estate in the village design.

Above average group: they are to use the OS map keys for reference, and must show on their design how the settlement is connected to other places – by roads, pathways, tracks etc. If appropriate, they could also give some indication of the height of the land in different parts of their settlement, using simple pencil contour lines.

Resources
- whiteboards or pieces of paper and pens
- a selection of OS maps
- a sheet of basic map symbols
- A3 sheets of paper marked with a river and a key box.

Cross-curricular links
History – invaders and settlers

Literacy – speaking and listening

Citizenship – sustaining environments

IT – drawing packages for map design.

Further ideas for developing this unit

This section provides some extra activities which help to develop the unit further. In particular, they encourage children to use maps and atlases to find out information. These activities can be used within the lessons suggested, or used to re-visit the topic at a later date. They also provide some ideas for fieldwork, which could be carried out in the local area at an appropriate time.

1. **Children take part in group role-play**, in which they play the roles of new settlers arriving in the UK. As a group they are given two or three options for a settlement site, and they have to come to a group decision as to which one is most suitable. Different characters will have different interests: for example, those responsible for house-building will consider wood and building material supplies, while others may be more concerned about defence. Each settler has to put their point across to the group.

2. **Identify two localities on a map** – if possible, one in the local area and one some distance away. Compare the two locations in terms of features, and list similarities and differences. Look at photographs of these places and ask the children to describe what they see, making sure they only use evidence from the photographs – e.g. 'What does the picture tell you about the landscape/soil/weather/occupations of people in this place?' Draw sketches from the photographs to show the main features. Visit the local settlement and carry out a land-use study, presenting findings using ICT. Make contact with a school in the other locality, and compare the results of the land-use surveys.

3. Using a **road atlas** of the UK (or Europe, for a more challenging activity):

   Ask the children, in pairs, to plan a route between two destinations
   - by motorways
   - by road.

   Measure the distance between the places, and work out the time it might take to get there. Think about average travel speeds, the need to stop, etc. The legal road speeds are printed in the atlas (either at the front or the back).

   Pose questions such as:
   - Why does a journey sometimes take longer than planned?
   - How can you find out about traffic information and road conditions?

   Identify places to stop, and features or sites to see. Use the internet to look up these places, using a search engine, and plan a short visit to one of them. What might you see or do there?

4. Many of the activities lend themselves to **fieldwork**; for example:
   - Look at the settlement in your local area on the map, and then go out to see if the original reasons for its development (a) can still be found and (b) are still important.
   - Find how many different routes link two places in your area, e.g. main road, small road, track, footpath etc. Which came first? Which is quickest? Which is the most useful, and to whom?

5. Using a **map of the UK** or **world** as appropriate:

   Carry out a **survey of where the people in your school live**. This could be by country, town or type of settlement, for example:
   - Town centre
   - Suburban area
   - Village
   - Isolated settlement, e.g. a farm.

   Plot the results on a graph and discuss the findings. Compare this with results from another class. What interesting things do you notice? Where do most people live?

   Ask a number of people where they would most like to live and why. Is there a difference between the answers given by those at school and adults? Can you think of reasons why this might be?

6. Look at **modern-day settlers**

   In small groups, discuss why people move and re-settle, e.g. change of jobs, change of personal circumstances, moving nearer to family.

   Identify pupils in the school or adults known to the school (and willing to take part) who have moved recently, and interview them to find out where they have come from. Locate these places on a map. Complete a table and graph to show the distances moved by individuals.

   Decide on questions to ask these individuals; for example, What is similar or different about the place you have moved from compared with here? What about the services, shops etc?

   Interviews give the opportunity to use a range of technology, such as tape recorders, video cameras and digital cameras, where appropriate.

7. **The future**

   Ask the children to think about where they would move to if they had the choice. What are their reasons, and what sort of place would they want it to be? Is there a perfect place to move to, or do we have to make compromises? How do we eventually make our decisions?

SuperSchemes | Unit 9: Village settlers

Using the activities

Activity sheet 1

Photocopy or print the page from the CD and cut out the cards. The aim of this activity is to encourage the children to discuss the relative merits of each of the locations as a possible settlement site. The two features described on each card are the dominant ones in each place. Children can either work in pairs or in a small group.

Pose the question 'Which location would be the best site to settle in?' The children have to discuss the choices available on the limited information given. They can place them in order of merit and comment on their choices. The card with the settlement already shown should raise the question 'Can this area support any more settlement?'

Activity sheet 2

The strips can be cut up according to how they are to be used. This means the activity can be differentiated in several different ways:

- Leave the strip with the symbols on intact. Cut up the other two strips so that the pictures and names can be matched to the first strip.
- Another version is to leave the first two strips intact and match only the names.
- The whole template can be kept intact and a second copy cut up, allowing the children to cover up the template symbols with the matching ones.
- Children can be asked to work out their own game using the activity.

Activity sheet 3

This activity is an assessment task: the objective is to allow children to show how much they have learned about the changing nature of settlement over time.

The empty boxes are provided for children to describe the settlement features in each box and to comment on how the scenes change over the centuries. Which features remain constant? What sort of challenges might the people in these places have faced?

The final box encourages the children to think about how this settlement might look towards the end of the 21st century. What would be a major change? What might stay the same?

This activity might benefit from the children having had some 'futures' debate, possibly about their own locality. On the other hand the activity could be used as an introduction, to identify those children who are able to think out the issues and challenges which will face settlements in the future. Discussion could then be used as follow-up work.

Activity sheet 4

You will need a range of story books with pictures or text about places, buildings or different locations. Many story books are based on a settlement of some type. This activity asks the children to identify homes or settlements which form a backdrop to the story, and to talk about what they are like. The activity might also provide an opportunity for children to look at settlements in other parts of the world and debate why they might have been located where they are.

Further questions you could ask the children are:

- Why do you think this place grew up here?
- How does this place/building compare with where you live?
- Can you describe what the buildings are being used for?
- What are the buildings made from?
- Is this place a city, town or village? How do you know?

Activity sheet 5

You will need advertisements for houses for sale or new housing developments. These are readily found in your local newspaper or the better quality Sunday newspapers, or there may be housing developments in your area with sales brochures available. Children can work in pairs or individually. This activity is also useful for homework, as most children will have local papers available at home.

The activity asks the children to investigate the information provided about the places for sale, and to recognise some of the persuasive language used: 'highly sought-after', 'deceptively spacious', 'excellent local amenities' and 'architect-designed' are examples of phrases which children will recognise as persuasive language. You might also ask children to:

- visit the developer's website and look at the plans
- identify the factors which have influenced the location – is it near a motorway, or a train station, or schools and shops?
- discuss whether they would like to live here and why
- find out if the illustrations are photographs of real buildings, or artist's impressions, and discuss why this makes a difference.

Activity sheet 1: Which location?

A

- woodland
- lowland area near river

B

- high land
- fertile soil

C

- river/bridging point
- undulating land

D

- woodland
- established settlement

SuperSchemes | Unit 9: Village settlers

Super Schemes

Village settlers *by Paula Richardson and Emma Till*

The place where we live and work is intensely interesting to all of us; children, 80% of whom live or go to school in an urban or suburban area, are fascinated by the nature of the built environment with which they have daily contact. It is easy, therefore, to engage their interest in finding out how that place came to be the way it is, and they are often surprised to learn that the place they know, with its modern buildings and complex road systems, had its location fixed in the landscape many centuries ago.

This unit explores the reasons for the establishment of original settlements, and examines the factors that influence the choices made. It then moves on to develop these ideas with activities which ask children to use maps and a range of other resources to examine more recent settlements, and to look at the complexity of factors which have resulted in their location. Children are also encouraged to think about the 'futures scenario' by looking at future settlement planning and how personal circumstances affect people's decisions about where to live.

Paula Richardson is an education adviser, teacher and author of many books as well as some of the original QCA Schemes of Work.

Emma Till is a teacher and author, and acts as a consultant for QCA in geography.

© Geographical Association, 2005

This book is copyright under the Berne Convention. All rights are reserved. Apart from any fair dealing for the purpose of private study, research, criticism or review, as permitted under the Copyright, Designs and Patents Act 1988, no part of this publication may be reproduced, stored in a retrieval system, or transmitted in any form or by any means, electronic, electrical, chemical, mechanical, optical, photocopying, recording or otherwise, without the prior written permission of the copyright owner. Enquiries should be addressed to the Geographical Association. As a benefit of membership GA members may reproduce material for their own internal school/departmental use, provided that the GA holds copyright. The views expressed in this publication are those of the author and do not necessarily represent those of the Geographical Association.

ISBN 1 84377 142 X

First published 2005

Impression number 10 9 8 7 6 5 4 3 2 1

Year 2008 2007 2006

Published by the **Geographical Association**
160 Solly Street, Sheffield S1 4BF.
The Geographical Association is a registered charity: no 313129.

Design concept: **Bryan Ledgard**
Design: **Ledgard Jepson Ltd**
Copy editing: **Asgard Publishing Services**
Maps: **Paul Coles**
Illustrations: **Linzi Henry**
Acknowledgements and photo credits can be found on the CD
Printed and bound in England by Henry Ling Ltd, The Dorset Press

SuperSchemes

Each unit in the SuperSchemes series comprises a booklet, a CD and a regularly updated website area:

Unit 1 Around our school: The seagulls' busy day *Colin Bridge*
Unit 2 Making our area safer: The twins on holiday *Colin Bridge*
Unit 3 An island home *Liz Lewis*
Unit 4 Seaside selections *John Halocha and Vanessa Richards*
Unit 5 The world comes to Barnaby Bear! *Elaine Jackson*
Unit 6 Investigating the local area: Our street *Rachel Bowles*
Unit 7 Hot, cold, wet, dry? *Margaret Mackintosh*
Unit 8 Improving the environment: Access for all *Simon Catling*
Unit 9 Village settlers *Paula Richardson and Emma Till*
Unit 10 A village in India *Jo Price*
Unit 11 Water *Pam Copeland and Des Bowden*
Unit 12 Looking at Europe *Paula Richardson and Emma Till*
Unit 13 A contrasting UK locality: Where do you want to go today? *Paula Owens*
Unit 14 Investigating rivers *Andrew Turney*
Unit 15 The mountain environment *Tony Richardson*
Unit 16 What's in the news? *Kate Russell*
Unit 17 Global Eye *Tony Richardson*
Unit 18 Connections: Integrating ICT into geography *Wendy Garner and Tony Pickford*
Unit 19 Where we go, what we do *Margaret Mackintosh*
Unit 20 Geography and culture *Emma Till*
Unit 21 Improving the view from our window *Sue Parsons*
Unit 22 A contrasting overseas locality: The Gambia *Pam Copeland and Des Bowden*
Unit 23 Investigating coasts *Tony Pickford*
Unit 24 Passport to the world *Larraine Poulter*
Unit 25 Geography and numbers *Paul Baker*
Unit 26 Investigating the local area: Our town *Rachel Bowles*

The Geographical Association, 160 Solly Street, Sheffield S1 4BF
tel 0114 296 0088   fax 0114 296 7176
www.geography.org.uk   www.geographyshop.org.uk

ISBN 1-84377-142-X
9 781843 771425